MICHAEL
FOREMAN'S
PLAYTIME
RHYMES

To my children and their children

MICHAEL FOREMAN'S
❖ PLAYTIME RHYMES ❖

WALKER BOOKS
AND SUBSIDIARIES
LONDON • BOSTON • SYDNEY • AUCKLAND

Rock-a-bye baby on the tree top,
When the wind blows the cradle will rock;
When the bough breaks the cradle will fall,
And down will come baby, cradle and all.

Two little eyes
    to look around,
Two little ears to
    hear each sound;
One little nose to
    smell what's sweet,
One little mouth
    that likes to eat.

Here are my ears.
Here is my nose.

Here are my fingers.
Here are my toes.

Here are my eyes,
Both open wide.

Here is my mouth
With white teeth inside.

Here is my tongue
That helps me to speak.

Here is my chin,
And here are my cheeks.

Here are my hands
That help me to play.

Here are my feet,
For walking today.

Round and round the garden, like a teddy bear, one step, two step, tickle you under there!

This little piggy went to the market,
This little piggy stayed at home,
This little piggy had roast beef,
This little piggy had none.
This little piggy
went...
Wee,
wee,
wee,
all
the
way
home!

This is little Tommy Thumb,
Round and smooth as any plum.
This is busy Peter Pointer.
Surely he's a double-jointer.
This is mighty Toby Tall.
He's the biggest one of all.
This is dainty Reuben Ring.
He's too fine for anything.
And this little wee one, maybe,
Is the pretty Finger Baby.

Fee, fi, fo, fum,
See my finger,
See my thumb.
Fee, fi, fo, fum,
Finger's gone.
So is thumb.

13

Dance, Thumbkin, dance,
Dance, Thumbkin, dance.
Thumbkin cannot dance alone,
So dance you merry men
    every one.
Dance, Thumbkin, dance.

Dance, Pointer, dance,
Dance, Pointer, dance.
Pointer cannot dance alone,
So dance you merry men
    every one.
Dance, Pointer, dance.

Dance, Longman, dance,
Dance, Longman, dance.
Longman cannot dance alone,
So dance you merry men
    every one.
Dance, Longman, dance.

Dance, Ringman, dance,
Dance, Ringman, dance.
Ringman cannot dance alone,
So dance you merry men
every one.
Dance, Ringman, dance.

Dance, Baby, dance,
Dance, Baby, dance.
Baby cannot dance alone,
So dance you merry men
every one.
Dance, Baby, dance.

15

This is the way the ladies ride,
Nimble nim, nimble nim, nimble nan.

This is the way the gentlemen ride,
Gallop a trot!
Gallop a trot!
Gallop a trot!

Horsey, horsey, don't you stop.
Just let your feet go clippity clop.
Your tail go swish, your feet go round.
Giddy-up, we're homeward bound.

16

This is the way the farmers ride,
Jiggety jog, jiggety jog,
jiggety jog.

This is the way the butcher boy rides,
Tripperty trot, tripperty trot, tripperty trot.
Till he falls in a ditch with a flipperty flop,

Flipperty flop,
flop, flop!

I had a little nag that trotted up and down
I bridled him, and saddled him, and trotted out of town.

A farmer went trotting
upon his grey mare;
Bumpety, bumpety, bump!
With his daughter behind him,
so rosy and fair;
Lumpety, lumpety, lump!

A raven cried, "Croak",
and they all tumbled down;
Bumpety, bumpety, bump!
The mare broke her knees,
and the farmer his crown;
Lumpety, lumpety, lump!

The mischievous raven
flew laughing away;
Bumpety, bumpety, bump!
And vowed he would serve them the
same the next day;
Bumpety, bumpety, bump!

18

Bumpity, bumpity, bumpity, bump,
As if I was riding my charger,
Bumpity, bumpity, bumpity, bump,
As proud as an Indian rajah.
Hey, hey, clear the way,
Here comes the galloping major!

Ride away, ride away,
Johnny shall ride,
He shall have a pussy cat
Tied to one side;
He shall have a little dog
Tied to the other,
And Johnny shall ride
To see his grandmother.

Knock at the door,
Pull the bell,
Lift the latch,
And walk in.

Ring the bell,
Knock at the door,
Peep in,
Lift the latch,
Walk in,
Go way down cellar
And eat apples.

Here is the church,
And here's the steeple,
Open the doors,
And see all the people.

Here is the parson
Going upstairs,
And here's the parson
Saying his prayers.

21

Dem bones, dem bones dem dry bones
Dem bones, dem bones dem dry bones
Dem bones, dem bones dem dry bones
Now hear the word of the Lord!

The toe bone's connected to the foot bone
The foot bone's connected to the ankle bone
The ankle bone's connected to the leg bone
Now hear the word of the Lord!

Dem bones, dem bones gonna walk around, Dem bones, dem bones gonna walk around,

22

The leg bone's connected to the thigh bone
The thigh bone's connected to the hip bone
The hip bone's connected to the back bone
Now hear the word of the Lord!

The back bone's connected to the shoulder bone
The shoulder bone's connected to the neck bone
The neck bone's connected to the head bone
Now hear the word of the Lord!

Dem bones, dem bones gonna walk around, Now hear the word of the Lord!

23

You put your right arm in,
Your right arm out,
Your right arm in,
And you shake it all about,
You do the Hokey Cokey,
And you turn around,
That's what it's all about.

Oh, the Hokey, Cokey, Cokey!
Oh, the Hokey, Cokey, Cokey!
Oh, the Hokey, Cokey, Cokey!
Knees bend,
Arms stretch,
Ra! Ra! Ra!

You put your left arm in,
Your left arm out,
Your left arm in,
And you shake it all about,
You do the Hokey Cokey,
And you turn around,
That's what it's all about.

Oh, the Hokey, Cokey...

You put your right leg in,
Your right leg out,
Your right leg in,
And you shake it all about,
You do the Hokey Cokey,
And you turn around,
That's what it's all about.

Oh, the Hokey, Cokey…

You put your left leg in,
Your left leg out,
Your left leg in,
And you shake it all about,
You do the Hokey Cokey,
And you turn around,
That's what it's all about.

Oh, the Hokey, Cokey…

You put your whole self in,
Your whole self out,
Your whole self in,
And you shake it all about,
You do the Hokey Cokey,
And you turn around,
That's what it's all about.

Oh, the Hokey, Cokey…

Head, shoulders, knees and toes, knees and toes,
Head, shoulders, knees and toes, knees and toes,
And eyes and ears and mouth and nose,
Head, shoulders, knees and toes, knees and toes.

If you're happy and you know it, clap your hands.
If you're happy and you know it, clap your hands.
If you're happy and you know it,
And you really want to show it,
If you're happy and you know it, clap your hands.

If you're happy and you know it, stamp your feet,
If you're happy and you know it, stamp your feet,
If you're happy and you know it,
And you really want to show it,
If you're happy and you know it, stamp your feet.

If you're happy and you know it, shout "we are",
If you're happy and you know it, shout "we are",
If you're happy and you know it,
And you really want to show it,
If you're happy and you know it, shout

"We are".

The Farmer's in the Den,
The Farmer's in the Den,
Eee-Aye-Eee-Aye,
The Farmer's in the Den.

The Farmer wants a Wife,
The Farmer wants a Wife,
Eee-Aye-Eee-Aye,
The Farmer wants a Wife.

The Wife wants a Child,
The Wife wants a Child,
Eee-Aye-Eee-Aye,
The Wife wants a Child.

The Child wants a Nurse,
The Child wants a Nurse,
Eee-Aye-Eee-Aye,
The Child wants a Nurse.

The Nurse wants a Dog,
The Nurse wants a Dog,
Eee-Aye-Eee-Aye,
The Nurse wants a Dog.

The Dog wants a Bone,
The Dog wants a Bone,
Eee-Aye-Eee-Aye,
The Dog wants a Bone.

We all pat the Bone,
We all pat the Bone,
Eee-Aye-Eee-Aye,
We all pat the Bone.

Ring-a-ring o' roses, a pocket full of posies,
A-tishoo! A-tishoo! We all fall down.

The cows are in the meadow, eating buttercups,
A-tishoo! A-tishoo! We all get up.

The cows are in the meadow, eating all the grass,
A-tishoo! A-tishoo! Who's up last?

Not me!

Here we go round the mulberry bush,
The mulberry bush, the mulberry bush,
Here we go round the mulberry bush,
On a cold and frosty morning.

This is the way we wash our face,
Wash our face, wash our face,
This is the way we wash our face,
On a cold and frosty morning.

This is the way we brush our hair,
Brush our hair, brush our hair,
This is the way we brush our hair,
On a cold and frosty morning.

This is the way we clean our teeth,
Clean our teeth, clean our teeth,
This is the way we clean our teeth,
On a cold and frosty morning.

I'm a little snowman, short and fat
Here's my scarf and here's my hat
Pebbles for my buttons, carrot for my nose
Made of snow from head to toes.

Okki-tokki-unga,
Okki-tokki-unga,
Hey, Missa Day,
Missa Doh,
Missa Day,
Okki-tokki-unga,
Okki-tokki-unga,
Hey, Missa Day,
Missa Doh,
Missa Day.

Hexa cola misha woni,
Hexa cola misha woni,
Hexa cola misha woni.

34

If I were a bear, and a big bear too,
I shouldn't much care, if it froze or snew;
I shouldn't much mind if it snowed or friz –
I'd be all fur lined with a coat like his.
For I'd have fur boots and a brown fur wrap
And brown fur knickers and a big fur cap
I'd have a fur muffle-ruff to cover my jaws
And brown fur mittens on my big brown paws
With a big brown furry-down up to my head
I'd sleep all the winter in a big fur bed.

35

There was a man lived in the moon, lived in the moon, lived in the moon,
There was a man lived in the moon, and his name was Aiken Drum.

He played upon a ladle and his name was Aiken Drum.
He played upon a ladle and his name was Aiken Drum.

And he played upon a teacup, teacup, teacup,
And he played upon a teacup, and his name was Aiken Drum.
And he played upon a saucepan lid, a saucepan lid, a saucepan lid,
He played upon a saucepan lid and his name was Aiken Drum.

I am the music man,
I come from far away,
And I can play.
What can you play?
I play piano.

Pi-a, pi-a, pi-a-no, Piano, piano,
Pi-a, pi-a, pi-a-no,
Pi-a, piano.

I am a music man,
I come from far away,
And I can play.
What can you play?
I play the big drum.

Boom-di, boom-di, boom-di-boom,
Boom-di-boom, boom-di-boom,
Boom-di, boom-di, boom-di-boom,
Boom-di, boom-di-boom.

Pi-a, pi-a, pi-a-no, Piano, piano,
Pi-a, pi-a, pi-a-no, Pi-a, piano.

I am a music man,
I come from far away,
And I can play.
What can you play?
I play the trumpet.

Toot-ti, toot-ti, toot-ti-toot,
Toot-ti-toot, toot-ti-toot,
Toot-ti, toot-ti, toot-ti-toot,
Toot-ti, toot-ti-toot.

Boom-di, boom-di, boom-di-boom,
Boom-di-boom, boom-di-boom,
Boom-di, boom-di, boom-di-boom,
Boom-di, boom-di-boom.

Pi-a, pi-a, pi-a-no,
Piano, piano,
Pi-a, pi-a, pi-a-no,
Pi-a, piano.

Oh, we can play on the big bass drum,
And this is the music to it;
Boom, boom, boom
　　　　　goes the big bass drum.
And that's the way we do it.

Oh, we can play on the tambourine,
And this is the music to it;
Chink, chink, chink
　　　　　goes the tambourine
Boom, boom, boom goes the big bass drum.
And that's the way we do it.

40

Oh, we can play on the castanets,
And this is the music to it;
Click, clickety-click
go the castanets
Chink, chink, chink goes the tambourine
Boom, boom, boom goes the big bass drum.
And that's the way we do it.

Oh, we can play on the triangle,
And this is the music to it;
Ping, ping, ping
goes the triangle
Click, clickety-click go the castanets
Chink, chink, chink goes the tambourine
Boom, boom, boom goes the big bass drum.
And that's the way we do it.

41

This old man, he played **one**,
He played nick nack on my thumb.
With a nick nack paddy whack,
    give a dog a bone,
This old man came rolling home.

This old man, he played **two**,
He played nick nack on my shoe.
With a nick nack paddy whack,
    give a dog a bone,
This old man came rolling home.

This old man, he played **three**,
He played nick nack on my knee.
With a nick nack paddy whack,
   give a dog a bone,
This old man came rolling home.

This old man, he played **four**,
He played nick nack on my floor.
With a nick nack paddy whack,
   give a dog a bone,
This old man came rolling home.

43

This old man, he played five,
He played nick nack making a dive.
With a nick nack paddy whack,
  give a dog a bone,
This old man came rolling home.

44

This old man, he played six,
He played nick nack with some sticks.
With a nick nack paddy whack,
    give a dog a bone,
This old man came rolling home.

This old man, he played seven,
He played nick nack up in heaven.
With a nick nack paddy whack,
    give a dog a bone,
This old man came rolling home.

One man went to mow,
Went to mow a meadow.
One man
and his dog
Went to mow a meadow.

Two men went to mow,
Went to mow a meadow.
Two men,
one man
and his dog
Went to mow a meadow.

Three men went to mow,
Went to mow a meadow.
Three men,
two men,
one man
and his dog
Went to mow a meadow.

Four men went to mow,
Went to mow a meadow.
Four men,
three men,
two men,
one man
and his dog
Went to mow a meadow.

Five men went to mow,
Went to mow a meadow.
Five men,
four men,
three men,
two men,
one man
and his dog
Went to mow a meadow.

Six men went to mow,
Went to mow a meadow.
Six men,
five men,
four men,
three men,
two men,
one man
and his dog
Went to mow a meadow.

Seven men went to mow,
Went to mow a meadow.
Seven men,
six men,
five men,
four men,
three men,
two men,
one man
and his dog
Went to mow a meadow.

Eight men went to mow,
Went to mow a meadow.
Eight men,
seven men,
six men,
five men,
four men,
three men,
two men,
one man
and his dog
Went to mow a meadow.

Nine men went to mow,
Went to mow a meadow.
Nine men,
 eight men,
  seven men,
   six men,
    five men,
     four men,
      three men,
       two men,
        one man
         and his dog
Went to mow a meadow.

Ten men went to mow,
Went to mow a meadow.
Ten men,
 nine men,
  eight men,
   seven men,
    six men,
     five men,
      four men,
       three men,
        two men,
         one man
          and his dog
Went to mow a meadow.

48

When all the cows were sleeping
And the sun had gone to bed,
Up jumped the scarecrow
And this is what he said:

I'm a dingle dangle scarecrow
With a flippy floppy hat!
I can shake my arms like this,
I can shake my legs like that!

When the cows were in the meadow
And the pigeons in the loft,
Up jumped the scarecrow
And whispered very soft:

I'm a dingle dangle scarecrow
With a flippy floppy hat!
I can shake my arms like this,
I can shake my legs like that!

When all the hens were roosting
And the moon behind a cloud,
Up jumped the scarecrow
And shouted very loud:

I'm a...

49

Old Macdonald had a farm, E-I-E-I-O.
And on that farm he had some cows, E-I-E-I-O.
With a moo-moo here, and a moo-moo there,
Here a moo, there a moo,
Everywhere a moo-moo,
Old Macdonald had a farm,

E-I-E-I-O.

Old Macdonald had a farm, E-I-E-I-O.
And on that farm he had some sheep, E-I-E-I-O.
With a baa-baa here, and a baa-baa there,
Here a baa, there a baa,
Everywhere a baa-baa,
Old Macdonald had a farm,

E-I-E-I-O.

Old Macdonald had a farm, E-I-E-I-O.
And on that farm he had some pigs, E-I-E-I-O.
With an oink-oink here, and an oink-oink there,
    Here an oink, there an oink,
    Everywhere an oink-oink,
    Old Macdonald had a farm,

E-I-E-I-O.

Old Macdonald had a farm, E-I-E-I-O.
And on that farm he had some ducks, E-I-E-I-O.
With a quack-quack here, and a quack-quack there,
    Here a quack, there a quack,
    Everywhere a quack-quack,
    Old Macdonald had a farm,

E-I-E-I-O.

Two fat gentlemen met in a lane,
Bowed most politely, bowed once again.
How do you do, how do you do,
And how do you do again?

Two thin ladies met in a lane,
Bowed most politely, bowed once again.
How do you do, how do you do,
And how do you do again?

Two tall policemen met in a lane,
Bowed most politely, bowed once again.
How do you do,
    how do you do,
And how do
    you do again?

Two small school boys met in a lane,
Bowed most politely, bowed once again.
How do you do, how do you do,
And how do you do again?

Two little babies met in a lane,
Bowed most politely, bowed once again.
How do you do, how do you do,
And how do you do again?

Mr Duck went out to walk,
One day in pleasant weather.
He met Mr Turkey on the way
And there they walked together.
"Gobble, gobble, gobble."
"Quack, quack, quack."
"Goodbye, goodbye."
And then they both walked back.

53

The wheels on the bus go round and round,
round and round, round and round.
The wheels on the bus go
round and round.
All day long.

The driver on the bus says
"Move along please,
Move along please,
move along please."
The driver on the bus says
"Move along please."
All day long.

The wipers on the bus go
swish, swish, swish,
Swish, swish, swish,
swish, swish, swish.
The wipers on the bus go
swish, swish, swish.
All day long.

The horn on the bus goes
beep! beep! beep!
Beep! beep! beep!
beep! beep! beep!
The horn on the bus goes
beep! beep! beep!
All day long.

The people on the bus go chat, chat, chat,
Chat, chat, chat, chat, chat, chat,
The people on the bus go chat, chat, chat.
All day long.

The children on the bus bump up and down
Up and down, up and down.
The children on the bus bump up and down,
All day long.

The wheels on the bus go round and round, round and round, round

The babies on the bus go "WAAH! WAAH! WAAH!
WAAH! WAAH! WAAH!, WAAH! WAAH! WAAH!"
The babies on the bus go "WAAH! WAAH! WAAH!"
All day long.

The mummies on the bus go "Shh, shh, shh.
Shh, shh, shh, shh, shh, shh."
The mummies on the bus go "Shh, shh, shh."
All day long.

and round. The wheels on the bus go round and round. All day long.   57

Down by the station, early in the morning,
See the little puffer trains, all in a row.
See the engine driver pull the little handle.
Toot toot, puff puff, off we go!

58

59

The big ship sails on the alley alley oh
Alley alley oh, alley alley oh.
The big ship sails on the alley alley oh
On the last day of September.

The captain said, "It will never never do
Never never do, never never do."
The captain said, "It will never never do"
On the last day of September.

The big ship sank to
    the bottom of the sea
The bottom of the sea,
    the bottom of the sea.
The big ship sank to
    the bottom of the sea
On the last day
    of September.

Row, row, row your boat gently down the stream,
Merrily, merrily, merrily, merrily, life is but a dream.

Row, row, row your boat gently to and fro,
If you see a lion, don't forget to roar!

Row, row, row your boat gently down the stream,
If you see a crocodile, don't forget to scream!
Aahhhhhhhhhhhhhhhhhh!

Walking through the jungle, What do you see?
Can you hear a noise? What could it be?

Ah well, I think it's a snake, Sss! Sss! Sss!
I think it is a snake, Sss! Sss! Sss!
I think it is a snake,
$\qquad$ Ssss! Sssss! Sssssss!

Looking for his tea.

The elephant goes like this, like that,
He's terribly big, and he's terribly fat,
He has no fingers, he has no toes,
But goodness gracious what a nose!

63

I went to the animal fair,
The birds and the beasts were there.
The big baboon
          by the light of the moon,
Was combing his auburn hair.
The monkey fell out of his bunk,
And slid down the elephant's trunk,
The elephant sneezed
     and fell on his knees,
          And that was
               the end
          of the
               monkey
                    monkey
          monkey
     monkey
               monkey
          monkey

65

There were **ten** in the bed
And the little one said,
"Roll over! Roll over!"
So they all rolled over
And one fell out.

There were **nine** in the bed
And the little one said,
"Roll over! Roll over!"
So they all rolled over
And one fell out.

There were **eight** in the bed
And the little one said,
"Roll over! Roll over!"
So they all rolled over
And one fell out.

There were **seven** in the bed
And the little one said,
"Roll over! Roll over!"
So they all rolled over
And one fell out.

There were **six** in the bed
And the little one said,
"Roll over! Roll over!"
So they all rolled over
And one fell out.

There were **five** in the bed
And the little one said,
"Roll over! Roll over!"
So they all rolled over
And one fell out.

There were **four** in the bed
And the little one said,
"Roll over! Roll over!"
So they all rolled over
And one fell out.

There were **three** in the bed
And the little one said,
"Roll over! Roll over!"
So they all rolled over
And one fell out.

There were **two** in the bed
And the little one said,
"Roll over! Roll over!"
So they both rolled over
And one fell out.

There was **one** in the bed,
And he said,
"Roll over! Roll over!"
So he rolled over
And he fell out.

There were **none** in the bed,
So *nobody* said,
"Roll over! Roll over!"

One elephant went out to play
Upon a spider's web one day.
He thought it such a tremendous stunt
That he called for another little elephant.

Two elephants went out to play
Upon a spider's web one day.
They thought it such a tremendous stunt
That they called for another little elephant.

Three elephants went out to play
Upon a spider's web one day.
The web went CREAK, the web went CRACK
And all of a sudden they all ran back.

70

Incey Wincey Spider climbed up the water spout.
Down came the rain and washed poor Incey out.
Out came the sun and dried up all the rain.
So Incey Wincey Spider climbed up the spout again.

71

The animals went in two by two, Hurrah! Hurrah!
The animals went in two by two, Hurrah! Hurrah!
The animals went in two by two,
The elephant and the kangaroo
And they all went into the ark,
For to get out of the rain.

The animals went in three by three,
Hurrah! Hurrah!
The animals went in three by three,
Hurrah! Hurrah!
The animals went in three by three,
The wasp, the ant and the bumble-bee
And they all went into the ark,
For to get out of the rain.

The animals went in four by four,
Hurrah! Hurrah!
The animals went in four by four,
Hurrah! Hurrah!
The animals went in four by four,
The great hippopotamus stuck in the door
And they all went into the ark,
For to get out of the rain.

The animals went in five by five, Hurrah! Hurrah!
The animals went in five by five, Hurrah! Hurrah!
The animals went in five by five,
By feeding each other they stayed alive
And they all went into the ark,
For to get out of the rain.

The animals went in six by six,
Hurrah! Hurrah!
The animals went in six by six,
Hurrah! Hurrah!
The animals went in six by six,
They turned out the monkey
because of his tricks
And they all went into the ark,
For to get out
of the rain.

73

The animals went in seven by seven,
Hurrah! Hurrah!
The animals went in seven by seven,
Hurrah! Hurrah!
The animals went in seven by seven,
The little pig thought
        he was going to heaven
And they all went into the ark,
For to get out of the rain.

The animals went in eight by eight,
Hurrah! Hurrah!
The animals went in eight by eight,
Hurrah! Hurrah!
The animals went in eight by eight,
The lions they were almost late
And they all went into the ark,
For to get out of the rain.

The animals went in nine by nine,
Hurrah! Hurrah!
The animals went in nine by nine,
Hurrah! Hurrah!
The animals went in nine by nine,
The penguins were rude
    and pushed into the line
And they all went into the ark,
For to get out of the rain.

The animals went in ten by ten,
Hurrah! Hurrah!
The animals went in ten by ten,
Hurrah! Hurrah!
The animals went in ten by ten,
The rooster looked splendid
    and so did the hen
And they all went into the ark,
For to get out of the rain.

When I was one I ate a bun
The day I went to sea;
I jumped aboard a sailing ship
And the captain said to me:
"We're going this-way, that-way,
Forwards and backwards, over the deep blue sea.
A bottle of rum to fill my tum
And that's the life for me."

Here is the sea, the wavy sea.
Here is a boat, and here is me.
And all the fishes down below,
Wriggle their tails and away they go.

77

American jump,
American jump,
One, two, three.
Under the water,
under the sea,
Catching fishes for my tea,
Dead,
Or alive,
Or round the world?

A sailor went to
sea, sea, sea,
To see what he could
see, see, see,
But all that he could
see, see, see,
Was the bottom
of the deep blue
sea, sea, sea.

78

One, two, three, four, five,
Once I caught a fish alive.
Six, seven, eight, nine, ten,
Then I let him go again.
Why did you let him go?
Because he bit my finger so.
Which finger did he bite?
This little finger on the right.

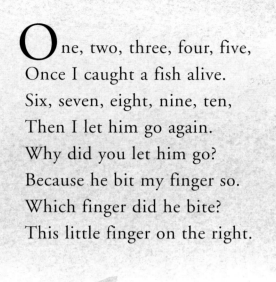

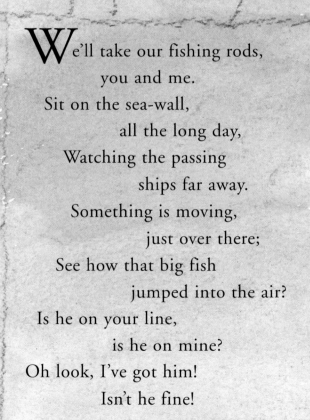

We'll take our fishing rods,
        you and me.
Sit on the sea-wall,
        all the long day,
Watching the passing
        ships far away.
Something is moving,
        just over there;
See how that big fish
        jumped into the air?
Is he on your line,
        is he on mine?
Oh look, I've got him!
        Isn't he fine!

Five little speckled frogs sat on a speckled log
Eating the most delicious grub, yum yum.
One jumped into the pool where he was
    nice and cool
And now there are four green speckled frogs,
    glub glub.

Four little speckled frogs sat on a speckled log
Eating the most delicious grub, yum yum.
One jumped into the pool where he was nice and cool
And now there are three green speckled frogs,
    glub glub.

Here's Mr Bullfrog
Sitting on a rock.
Along comes a little boy,
Mr Bullfrog jumps,
kerplop!

A little frog in a pond am I,
Hippity, hippity, hop.
And I can jump in the air so high,
Hippity, hippity, hop.

Three little speckled frogs sat on a speckled log
Eating the most delicious grub, yum yum.
One jumped into the pool where he was nice and cool
And now there are two green speckled frogs,
    glub glub.

Two little speckled frogs sat on a speckled log
Eating the most delicious grub, yum yum.
One jumped into the pool where he was
        nice and cool
And now there is one green speckled frog,
    glub glub.

One little speckled frog sat on a speckled log
Eating the most delicious grub, yum yum.
He jumped into the pool where he was
        nice and cool
And now there are no green speckled frogs,

glub glub.

Three little frogs asleep in the sun.
We'll creep up and wake them.
Then we will run.

There were two birds sat on a stone,
　Fa, la, la, la, lal, de;
One flew away, and then there was one,
　Fa, la, la, la, lal, de;
The other flew after, and then there was none,
　Fa, la, la, la, lal, de;
And so the poor stone was left all alone,
　Fa, la, la, la, lal, de!

Five little birds without any home,
　Five little trees in a row.
Come build your nests
In our branches tall,
We'll rock you to and fro.

82

In a cottage in a wood
   A little man at the window stood,
   Saw a rabbit hopping sore,
   Knocking at the door.
"Help me, help me, help me," he said.
"Or the hunter will shoot me dead!"
"Come, little rabbit, stay with me,
   Happy you will be."

83

If you go down to the woods today,
you're sure of a big surprise.
If you go down to the woods today,
you'd better go in disguise!

For every bear that ever there was
        will gather there for certain because
Today's the day the Teddy Bears have their picnic.

Every Teddy Bear who's been good is sure of a treat today.
There'll be lots of marvellous things to eat and wonderful games to play!
Beneath the trees where nobody sees,
        they'll hide-and-seek as long as they please,
Because that's the way the Teddy Bears have their picnic.

85

Picnic time for Teddy Bears,
    Those little Teddy Bears
    Are having a lovely time today.
Watch them, catch them unawares,
    And see them picnic on their holiday.
You'll see them gaily gad about,
    They love to play and shout,
    They never have any cares.

At six o'clock their mummies and daddies
    Will take them home to bed,
Because they're tired little Teddy Bears.

I'm a little teapot, short and stout,
Here's my handle, here's my spout.
When I see the teacups, hear me shout:
Tip me up and pour me out!

Jelly on the plate,
jelly on the plate,
wibble wobble wibble wobble,
jelly on the plate.

I eat my peas with honey.
I've done it all my life.
It makes the peas taste funny,
But it sticks them on the knife.

Five little peas in a pea-pod pressed,
One grew, two grew and so did all the rest.
They grew and grew and they did not stop,
Until all of a sudden the pod went ...

pop!

87

Ten fat sausages sizzling in the pan, ten fat sausages sizzling in the pan.

One went **pop!**

and another went **bang!**

There were eight fat sausages

sizzling in the pan.

88

Eight fat sausages sizzling in the pan,
Eight fat sausages sizzling in the pan.
One went pop! and another went bang!
There were six fat sausages sizzling in the pan.

Six fat sausages sizzling in the pan,
Six fat sausages sizzling in the pan.
One went pop! and another went bang!
There were four fat sausages sizzling in the pan.

Four fat sausages sizzling in the pan,
Four fat sausages sizzling in the pan.
One went pop! and another went bang!
There were two fat sausages sizzling in the pan.

Two fat sausages sizzling in the pan,
Two fat sausages sizzling in the pan.
One went pop! and another went bang!
There were no fat sausages sizzling in the pan.

Miss Polly had a dolly
Who was sick, sick, sick,
So she 'phoned for the doctor
To be quick, quick, quick.
The doctor came
With his bag and his hat,
And he rapped at the door
With a **rat-tat-tat.**

He looked at the dolly
And he shook his head.
Then he said, "Miss Polly,
Put her straight to bed."
He wrote on a paper
For a pill, pill, pill;
"I'll be back in the morning
With my **bill, bill, bill.**"

John Brown's baby got a cold upon his chest,
John Brown's baby got a cold upon his chest,
John Brown's baby got a cold upon his chest,
So they rubbed it with camphorated oil.

Camphor-amphor-amphor-ated,
Camphor-amphor-amphor-ated,
Camphor-amphor-amphor-ated,
So they rubbed it with camphorated oil.

91

Teddy bear, teddy bear, touch your toes,
Teddy bear, teddy bear, touch your nose,
Teddy bear, teddy bear, turn around,
Teddy bear, teddy bear, touch the ground.

Teddy bear, teddy bear, climb the stairs
Teddy bear, teddy bear, say your prayers
Teddy bear, teddy bear, turn out the light
Teddy bear, teddy bear, say goodnight.

Girls and boys, come out to play;
The moon doth shine as bright as day;
Leave your supper, and leave your sleep,
And come with your playfellows into the street.
Come with a whoop, come with a call,
Come with a good will or not at all,
A halfpenny roll will serve us all.
You find milk, and I'll find flour,
And we'll have a pudding in half-an-hour.

93

Hush, little baby, don't say a word,
  Papa's going to buy you a mockingbird.
And if that mockingbird don't sing,
  Papa's going to buy you a diamond ring.
And if that diamond ring turns to brass,
  Papa's going to buy you a looking-glass.
And if that looking-glass gets broke,
  Papa's going to buy you a billy-goat.
And if that billy-goat don't pull,
  Papa's going to buy you a cart and bull.
And if that cart and bull turn over,
  Papa's going to buy you a dog named Rover.
And if that dog named Rover don't bark,
  Papa's going to buy you a horse and cart.
And if that horse and cart fall down,
  You'll still be the sweetest little baby in the world.

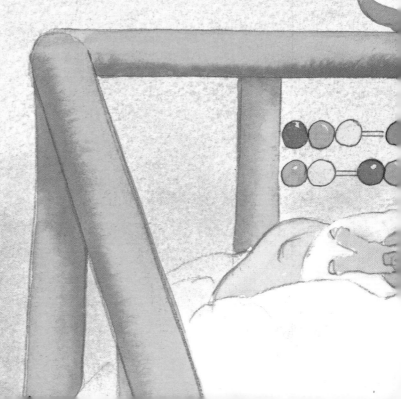

Golden slumbers kiss your eyes,
Smiles await you when you rise.
Sleep, pretty wantons, do not cry
And I will sing a lullaby:
Rock them, rock them, lullaby.

95

Sleep baby sleep
The father watches the sheep
The mother is shaking the dreamland tree
And softly a little dream falls on thee
Sleep, baby, sleep.

Baby's boat's a silver moon
　　Sailing in the sky,
Sailing o'er a sea of sleep
　　While the stars float by.

　　Sail, baby, sail
　　Out upon that sea;
Only don't forget to sail
　　Back again to me.

Baby's fishing for a dream,
　　Fishing far and near,
Her line a silver moonbeam is,
　　Her bait a silver star.

　　Sail, baby, sail
　　Out upon that sea;
Only don't forget to sail
　　Back again to me.

NOTES ABOUT THE RHYMES

THIS IS THE WAY THE LADIES RIDE ~ *Page 16*

For trotting rhymes like this put the baby on your knee and bounce it to the rhythm of the text.

KNOCK AT THE DOOR ~ *Page 20*

Knock on your forehead, pull your nose, lift your eyelid and point in your mouth.

RING THE BELL ~ *Page 20*

Pull your hair, knock on your forehead, lift your eyelid and open your mouth.

HERE IS THE CHURCH ~ *Page 21*

Lock your fingers together with your knuckles upwards and your fingers pointing down. On "Here is the steeple" raise

Here is the church

here is the steeple

open the doors

and here are the people

going upstairs

saying his prayers.

your index fingers to form a spire. Your thumbs are the church doors, open them and then to see the people flip your hands around and wiggle your fingers. To send the parson upstairs walk your fingers up the knuckles of your other hand. Put your palms together to say prayers.

HOKEY COKEY ~ *Page 24*

Everyone stands in a big circle, and puts their arm or leg into and out of the circle when it is mentioned. When "hokey cokey" is sung during the verse dance on the spot and then turn around. During the chorus, on "hokey cokey", everyone rushes to the middle and puts their arms in the air, rushes out and waves their arms in the air again!

THE FARMER'S IN THE DEN ~ *Page 28*

All the children join hands in a large circle, with the "farmer" in the middle. He or she chooses a wife, the wife chooses a child and so on, until everyone pats the child that has been chosen as the bone.

RING-A-RING O' ROSES ~ *Page 30*

Dance in a circle, sneeze, fall down, and then do the same for the next two verses.

HERE WE GO ROUND THE MULBERRY BUSH ~ *Page 31*

Dance in a circle during the chorus. Stand still during the verses and perform the actions.

I'M A LITTLE SNOWMAN ~ *Page 33*

Look stout, and point to the parts of clothing that are mentioned in the other verses.

OKKI-TOKKI-UNGA ~ *Page 34*

The actions to this rhyme tell the story of an Inuit going seal hunting in a kayak. "Okki-tokki-unga" is the chorus and "Hexa cola misha woni" is the verse. During the chorus swing your arms as if you are paddling a canoe. Repeat the verse four times: first time look for a seal, then harpoon the seal, and drag the seal into your boat. Finally, wave to someone on shore and roll the kayak over!

IF I WERE A BEAR ~ *Page 35*

Act out putting on the clothes and then going to bed.

AIKEN DRUM ~ *Page 36*

Either play the tune on the objects mentioned, or just pretend to.

I AM THE MUSIC MAN ~ *Page 38*

One child is the music man, and begins the song. Everyone else sings "What can you play?", the chorus, and also mimes the instruments as the music man describes them.

OH, WE CAN PLAY ~ *Page 40*

Mime the instruments mentioned in the rhyme.

ONE MAN WENT TO MOW ~ *Page 46*

A counting rhyme.

WHEN ALL THE COWS WERE SLEEPING ~ *Page 49*

Lie on the floor. When the scarecrow jumps up, you do too. Shake your head and your arms and legs when appropriate. Lie down again for the beginning of each new verse.

OLD MACDONALD HAD A FARM ~ *Page 50*

Keep repeating the song making as many different animal noises as you can think of.

TWO FAT GENTLEMEN ~ *Page 52*

The fat gentlemen are your thumbs. Bow them together, and then make the same action with the following finger at each verse.

MR DUCK ~ *Page 53*

Mr Duck is one thumb, and Mr Turkey is the other. Move them when they walk. Wobble Mr Turkey when he gobbles and quake Mr Duck when he quacks. When they say goodbye bow them together, and when they walk back move them apart.

THE WHEELS ON THE BUS ~ *Page 54*

Mime the actions and "chatter" by making mouth movements with your hands.

DOWN BY THE STATION ~ *Page 58*

Pull the handle, make the noises and mime the train's wheels turning.

ROW, ROW, ROW YOUR BOAT ~ *Page 62*

Face one another sitting on the floor, hold hands, and rock back and forth.

WALKING THROUGH THE JUNGLE ~ *PAGE 63*

Look, listen, and then make your arm wind like a snake while making hissing sounds.

THE ELEPHANT GOES LIKE THIS ~ *Page 63*

Sway heavily to each side, reach up to show how big he is, reach out to show how wide, point to your fingers and then your toes, and make your arm an elephant's trunk.

I WENT TO THE ANIMAL FAIR ~ *Page 65*

Mime the actions: comb your hair, sneeze, and fall on your knees. You may also clap rhythmically.

ONE ELEPHANT WENT OUT TO PLAY ~ *Page 70*

The first elephant walks around swinging its trunk, then chooses the second elephant who holds onto the first with his or her trunk, and so on until all the children are elephants walking in line attached by their trunks.

INCEY WINCEY SPIDER ~ *Page 71*

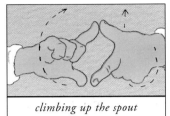  

climbing up the spout | *and washed ...* | *out came the sun.*

Climb the spout by alternating your forefingers and thumbs. Lower your hands while wiggling your fingers to show rain. Make a circle for the sun, then climb up the spout again.

THE ANIMALS WENT IN TWO BY TWO ~ *Page 72*

This is a counting rhyme – hold up fingers for each number.

WHEN I WAS ONE ~ *Page 76*

On "one" hold up a finger, on "bun" eat, and jump on "jumped". Sway on "this-way, that-way" and "Forwards and backwards". Pat your tum on "rum" and slap your thigh on "And that's the life for me".

A SAILOR WENT TO SEA ~ *Page 78*

There are two possible actions for this rhyme – hopping or clapping. Hop up and down on one leg with your hand

shading your eyes every time you say "see" or "sea". Two children can clap together in time to the rhyme, shading their eyes when they say "sea" or "see".

ONE, TWO, THREE, FOUR, FIVE ~ *Page 79*

Count each finger, pretend to catch a fish, count the fingers on the other hand and then throw the fish back. Shake your right hand when bitten and then show the little finger on the right hand.

FIVE LITTLE SPECKLED FROGS ~ *Page 80*

This is a finger rhyme – hold up five fingers, then four, and so on until all are gone.

A LITTLE FROG IN A POND AM I ~ *Page 80*

Hop like a frog.

THERE WERE TWO BIRDS SAT ON A STONE ~ *Page 82*

A finger rhyme – hide the fingers one at a time.

IN A COTTAGE IN A WOOD ~ *Page 83*

Perform the actions in the rhyme. First trace a window

In a cottage | *at the window stood* | *hopping* | *knocking*

frame and pretend to look out of the window wearing glasses. Hop your hand like a rabbit, knock at the door, throw your arms in the air for each "help me" and then

Help me!

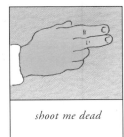

shoot me dead

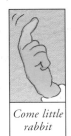

Come little rabbit

Happy you will be

make a shooting action. Beckon the rabbit into the house and finally stroke the rabbit in your arms.

JELLY ON THE PLATE ~ *Page 86*

Hold the child on your knee and wobble them from side to side.

I'M A LITTLE TEAPOT ~ *Page 86*

Put one hand on your hip, and crook the other arm into a spout. Lean over to pour.

I EAT MY PEAS WITH HONEY ~ *Page 87*

Mime eating.

FIVE LITTLE PEAS ~ *Page 87*

Make a fist and open out the fingers one by one. Clap loudly on "Pop".

TEN FAT SAUSAGES ~ *Page 88*

Clap loudly on "Pop!" and "Bang!"

MISS POLLY HAD A DOLLY ~ *Page 90*

Rock the sick baby and then telephone the doctor. Mime putting on the doctor's hat and knock on the door. Shake your head, waggle your finger, and write out a prescription. Wave goodbye at the end.

sick, sick, sick

… phoned for the doctor

… and his hat

… rapped at the door

… he shook his head

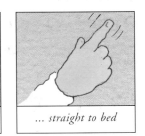

… straight to bed

… wrote on a paper

… back in the morning

JOHN BROWN'S BABY ~ *Page 91*

Sing the song six times. First time sing all the way through.

Thereafter omit a word each time and replace it with an

action. In the second verse mime rocking a baby instead of

singing "baby".

In the third verse cough quietly for "cold".

In the fourth verse tap your chest for "chest".

In the fifth verse rub your chest.

In the sixth verse hold your nose for "camphorated oil".

TEDDY BEAR, TEDDY BEAR ~ *Page 92*

Touch nose and toes as they are mentioned. Then mime

each action.

HUSH, LITTLE BABY ~ *Page 94*

This rhyme, and all those that follow,

are lullabies for rocking

your baby to sleep.

ACKNOWLEDGEMENTS

"Teddy Bears' Picnic" Words by Jimmy Kennedy and Music by
John W. Bratton © 1907, M. Witmark and Co. Ltd, USA.
Reproduced by permission of B. Feldman and Co. Ltd, London WC2H 0QY.

The Publishers have made every effort to ensure that the material in this book
is in the public domain. If an inadvertent breach of copyright has been made
the Publishers will be pleased to correct any omission in future editions.

First published 2002 by Walker Books Ltd
87 Vauxhall Walk, London SE11 5HJ

This edition published 2004

10 9 8 7 6 5 4 3 2 1

This selection © 2002 Walker Books Ltd

Illustrations © 2002 Michael Foreman

The right of Michael Foreman to be identified as illustrator
of this work has been asserted by him in accordance
with the Copyright, Designs and Patents Act 1988

This book has been typeset in Garamond

Printed in China

British Library Cataloguing in Publication Data:
a catalogue record for this book is available from the British Library

ISBN 1-84428-495-6

www.walkerbooks.co.uk

INDEX OF FIRST LINES